SACRED CHRISTMAS DUETS

8 CHERISHED CAROLS FOR ONE PIANO, FOUR HANDS

— PIANO LEVEL —
INTERMEDIATE

ISBN 978-1-5400-5414-2

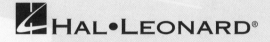

Visit Hal Leonard Online at
www.halleonard.com

Visit Phillip at
www.phillipkeveren.com

Contact us:
Hal Leonard
7777 West Bluemound Road
Milwaukee, WI 53213
Email: info@halleonard.com

In Europe, contact:
Hal Leonard Europe Limited
42 Wigmore Street
Marylebone, London, W1U 2RN
Email: info@halleonardeurope.com

In Australia, contact:
Hal Leonard Australia Pty. Ltd.
4 Lentara Court
Cheltenham, Victoria, 3192 Australia
Email: info@halleonard.com.au

PREFACE

When families and friends gather together at Christmas time, music is often an important part of the celebration. Whether in a recital, worship service, or simple evening at home, piano duets can provide a wonderful connection point for everyone. I have sweet memories of playing duets during the holidays, and I hope that these arrangements will help you make some special memories of your own.

So, find a duet partner and eighty-eight keys – and celebrate the season!

Merry Christmas,

BIOGRAPHY

Phillip Keveren, a multi-talented keyboard artist and composer, has composed original works in a variety of genres from piano solo to symphonic orchestra. He gives frequent concerts and workshops for teachers and their students in the United States, Canada, Europe, Australia, and Asia. Mr. Keveren holds a B.M. in composition from California State University Northridge and a M.M. in composition from the University of Southern California.

CONTENTS

THE FIRST NOEL

17th Century English Carol
Music from W. Sandys' *Christmas Carols*
Arranged by Phillip Keveren

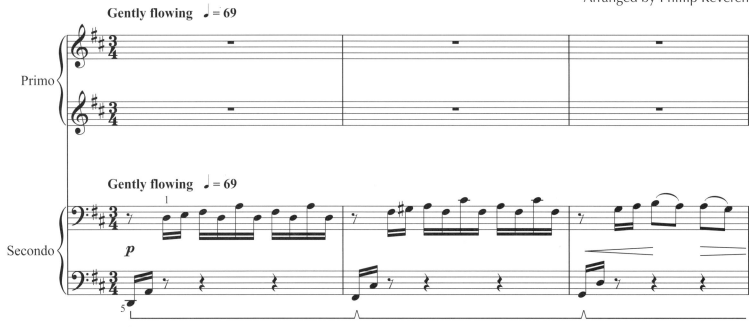

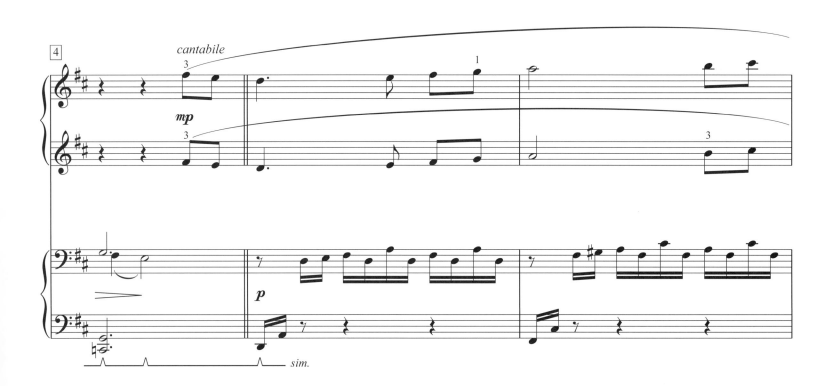

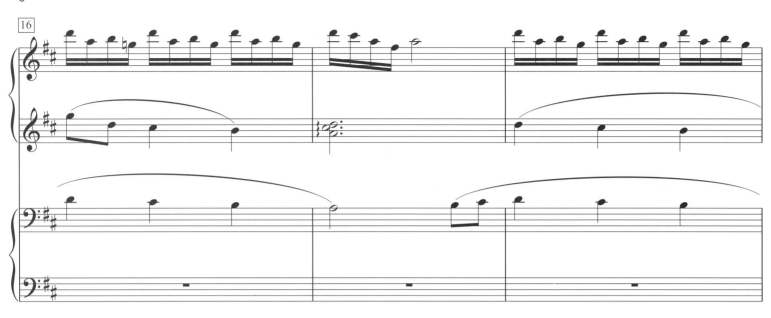

HARK! THE HERALD ANGELS SING

Words by CHARLES WESLEY
Altered by GEORGE WHITEFIELD
Music by FELIX MENDELSSOHN-BARTHOLDY
Arranged by Phillip Keveren

GO, TELL IT ON THE MOUNTAIN

African-American Spiritual
Verses by JOHN W. WORK, JR.
Arranged by Phillip Keveren

IT CAME UPON THE MIDNIGHT CLEAR

Words by EDMUND HAMILTON SEARS
Music by RICHARD STORRS WILLIS
Arranged by Phillip Keveren

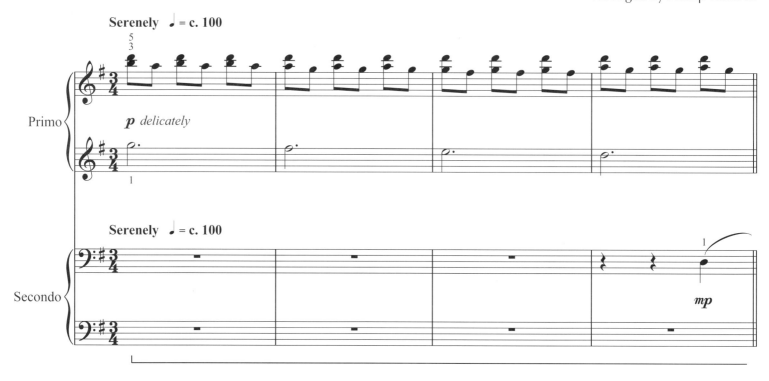

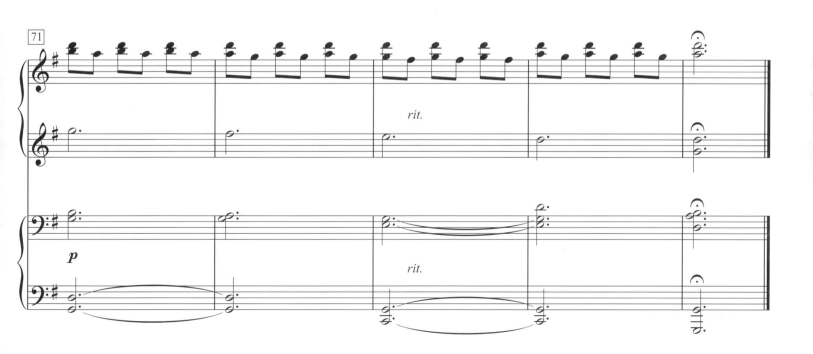

O COME, ALL YE FAITHFUL

Music by JOHN FRANCIS WADE
Latin Words translated by FREDERICK OAKELEY
Arranged by Phillip Keveren

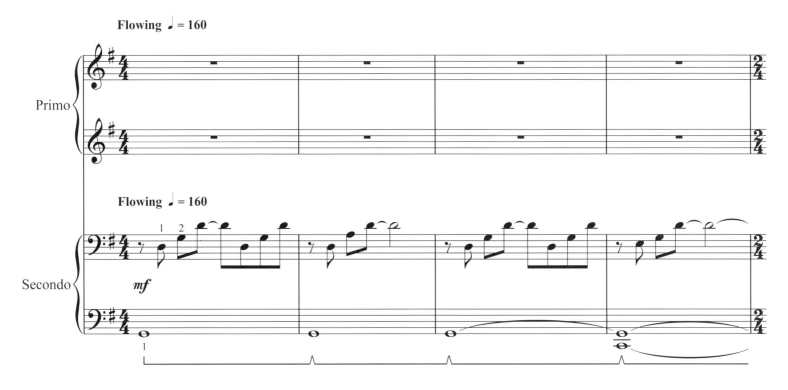

O HOLY NIGHT

French Words by PLACIDE CAPPEAU
English Words by JOHN S. DWIGHT
Music by ADOLPHE ADAM
Arranged by Phillip Keveren

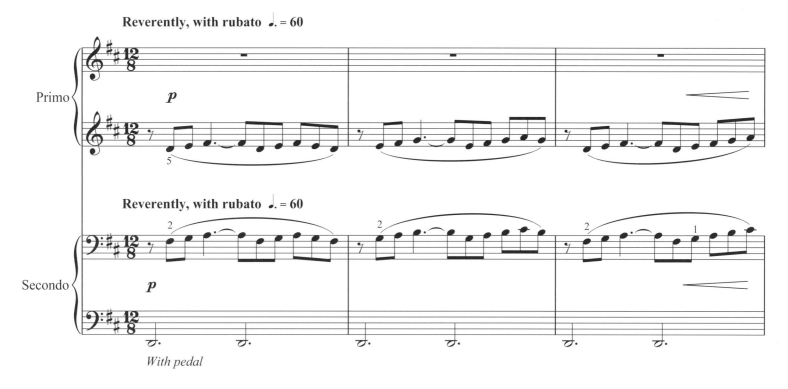

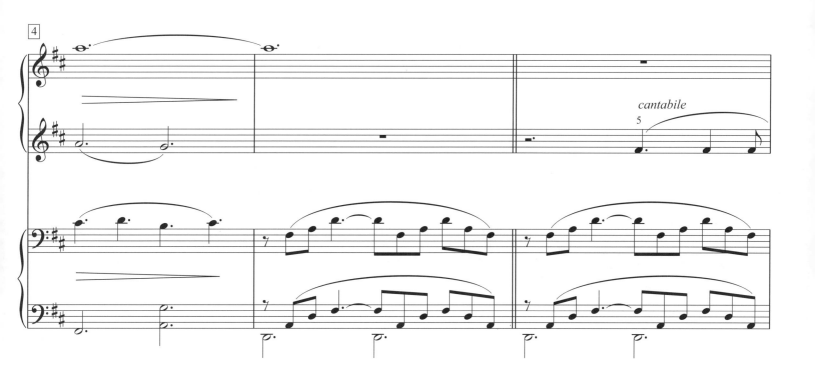

O COME, O COME, EMMANUEL

Traditional Latin Text
V. 1,2 translated by JOHN M. NEALE
V. 3,4 translated by HENRY S. COFFIN
15th Century French Melody
Arranged by Phillip Keveren

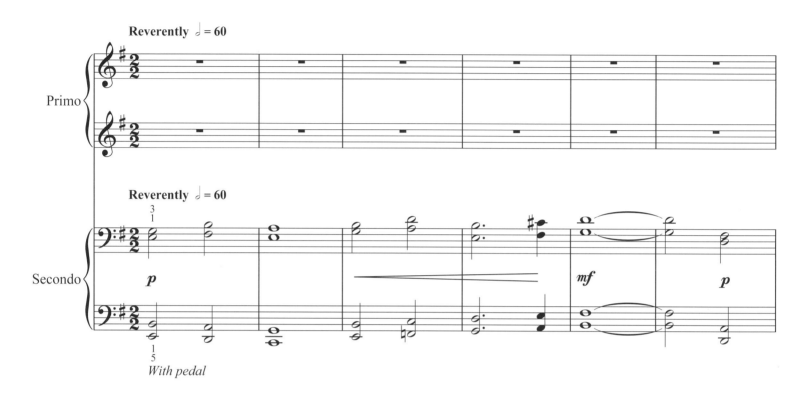

SILENT NIGHT

Words by JOSEPH MOHR
Translated by JOHN F. YOUNG
Music by FRANZ X. GRUBER
Arranged by Phillip Keveren

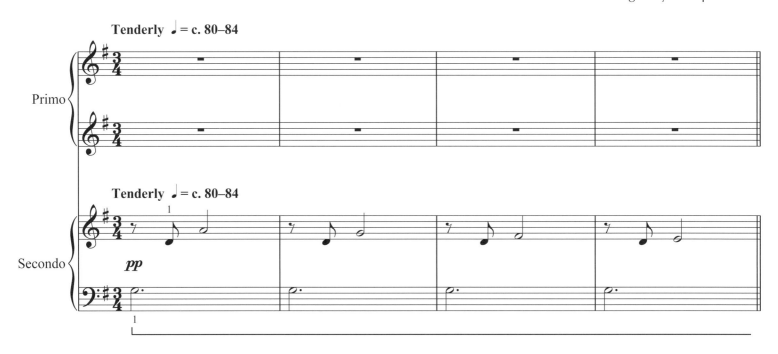

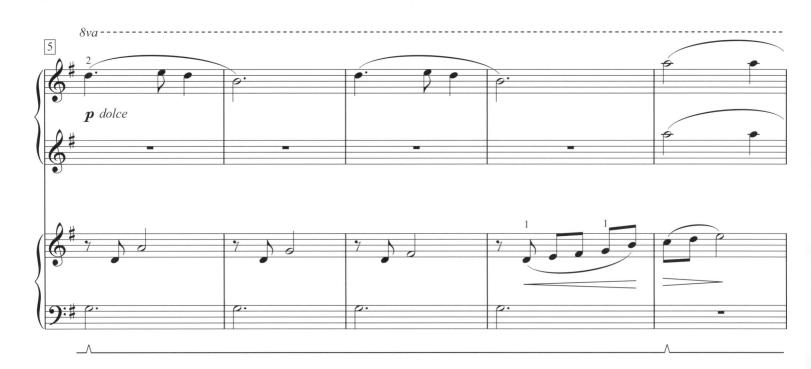

PIANO DUETS
IN THE PHILLIP KEVEREN SERIES

1 PIANO, 4 HANDS

THE CHRISTMAS VARIATIONS
Eight classic carol settings expertly arranged for piano duet by Phillip Keveren. Includes: Angels We Have Heard on High • Ding Dong! Merrily on High! • God Rest Ye Merry, Gentlemen • I Saw Three Ships • Joy to the World • Lo, How a Rose E'er Blooming • Still, Still, Still • We Wish You a Merry Christmas.
00126452 Piano Duet............$12.99

CLASSICAL THEME DUETS
Eight beloved masterworks masterfully arranged as early intermediate duets by Phillip Keveren. Includes: Bizet – Habanera • Borodin – Polovetsian Dance • Grieg – In the Hall of the Mountain King • Vivaldi – The Four Seasons ("Autumn") • and more.
00311350 Easy Piano Duets...$10.99

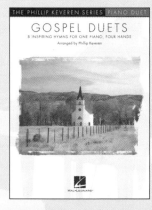

GOSPEL DUETS
Eight inspiring hymns arranged by Phillip Keveren for one piano, four hands, including: Church in the Wildwood • His Eye Is on the Sparrow • In the Garden • Just a Closer Walk with Thee • The Old Rugged Cross • Shall We Gather at the River? • There Is Power in the Blood • When the Roll Is Called up Yonder.
00295099 Piano Duet $12.99

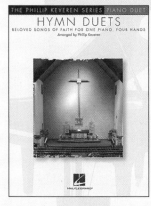

HYMN DUETS
12 beloved songs of faith: All Creatures of Our God and King • All Hail the Power of Jesus' Name • Fairest Lord Jesus • Holy, Holy, Holy • I Surrender All • Immortal, Invisible • It Is Well with My Soul • Joyful, Joyful, We Adore Thee • A Mighty Fortress Is Our God • O Sacred Head, Now Wounded • Praise to the Lord, the Almighty • Rejoice, the Lord Is King.
00311544 Piano Duet $12.99

PRAISE & WORSHIP DUETS
Eight worshipful duets by Phillip Keveren: As the Deer • Awesome God • Give Thanks • Great Is the Lord • Lord, I Lift Your Name on High • Shout to the Lord • There Is a Redeemer • We Fall Down.
00311203 Piano Duet $12.99

SACRED CHRISTMAS DUETS
Phillip Keveren has arranged eight beloved Christmas songs into duets perfect for holiday recitals or services. Includes: The First Noel • Go, Tell It on the Mountain • Hark! the Herald Angels Sing • It Came upon the Midnight Clear • O Come, All Ye Faithful • O Come, O Come, Emmanuel • O Holy Night • Silent Night.
00294755 Piano Duet............$12.99

STAR WARS
Eight intergalactic arrangements of *Star Wars* themes for late intermediate to early advanced piano duet, including: Across the Stars • Cantina Band • Duel of the Fates • The Imperial March (Darth Vader's Theme) • Princess Leia's Theme • Star Wars (Main Theme) • The Throne Room (And End Title) • Yoda's Theme.
00119405 Piano Duet $14.99

WORSHIP SONGS FOR TWO
Eight worship favorites arranged for one piano, four hands by Phillip Keveren. Songs include: Amazing Grace (My Chains Are Gone) • Cornerstone • Forever (We Sing Hallelujah) • Great I Am • In Christ Alone • The Lion and the Lamb • Lord, I Need You • 10,000 Reasons (Bless the Lord).
00253545 Piano Duet $12.99

www.halleonard.com